JOSEPH MIDTHUN   SAMUEL HITI

BUILDING BLOCKS OF MATHEMATICS

FRACTIONS

WORLD
BOOK

a Scott Fetzer company
Chicago
www.worldbook.com

World Book, Inc.
233 N. Michigan Avenue
Chicago, IL 60601
U.S.A.

For information about other World Book publications,
visit our website at www.worldbook.com
or call 1-800-WORLDBK (967-5325).
For information about sales to schools and libraries,
call 1-800-975-3250 (United States),
or 1-800-837-5365 (Canada).

Library of Congress Cataloging-in-Publication Data
Fractions.

    pages cm. -- (Building blocks of mathematics)
   Summary: "A graphic nonfiction volume that
introduces critical basic fraction concepts"-- Provided
by publisher.
   Includes index.
   ISBN 978-0-7166-1434-0 -- ISBN 978-0-7166-1475-3
(pbk.)
   1. Fractions--Comic books, strips, etc.--Juvenile
literature. 2. Graphic novels. I. World Book, Inc.
QA117.F697 2013
513.2'6--dc23
                        2012035464

Building Blocks of Mathematics
ISBN: 978-0-7166-1431-9 (set, hc.)

Printed in China by Shenzhen Donnelley
Printing Co., Ltd., Guangdong Province
2nd printing October 2013

Acknowledgments:
Created by Samuel Hiti and Joseph Midthun
Art by Samuel Hiti
Written by Joseph Midthun
Special thanks to Anita Wager, Hala Ghousseini,
and Syril McNally.

STAFF
Executive Committee
President: Donald D. Keller
Vice President and Editor in Chief:
   Paul A. Kobasa
Vice President, Sales & Marketing:
   Sean Lockwood
Vice President, International: Richard Flower
Director, Human Resources: Bev Ecker

Editorial
Manager, Series and Trade: Cassie Mayer
Writer and Letterer: Joseph Midthun
Manager, Contracts & Compliance
   (Rights & Permissions): Loranne K. Shields

Manufacturing/Pre-Press
Director: Carma Fazio
Manufacturing Manager: Steven Hueppchen
Production/Technology Manager:
   Anne Fritzinger
Proofreader: Emilie Schrage

Graphics and Design
Senior Manager, Graphics and Design: Tom Evans
Coordinator, Design Development and
   Production: Brenda B. Tropinski
Book Design: Samuel Hiti

TABLE OF CONTENTS

The number on top is called the numerator.

It tells you how many equal parts we are counting.

The bottom number is called the denominator.

It tells you how many equal parts the whole is divided into.

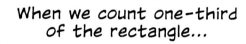

When we count one-third of the rectangle...

...we are counting 1 of the 3 equal parts.

1,   2,   3!

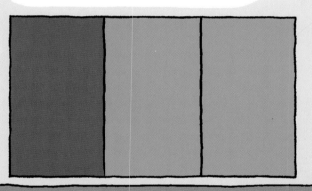

Writing fractions like this is okay, too...

...as long as the numerator and denominator are clearly separated by a line!

There are countless numbers of fractions!

Let's just focus on a few common ones.

A whole square!

$\frac{1}{2}$ is called a half.

Buzz

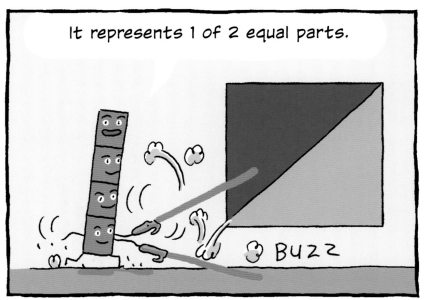

It represents 1 of 2 equal parts.

Buzz

Oh!

A whole circle!

Buzz

Take that!

Buzz

Buzz

Buzz

8

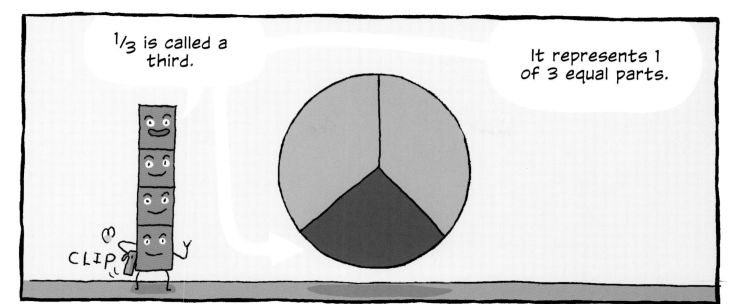

1/3 is called a third.

It represents 1 of 3 equal parts.

CLIP

Hey, a whole triangle!

Buzz

1/4 is called a fourth—

Buzz

Buzz

Buzz

Buzz

Also known as a quarter!

It represents 1 of 4 equal parts.

Tunk

Zwip

FRACTIONS ON A NUMBER LINE

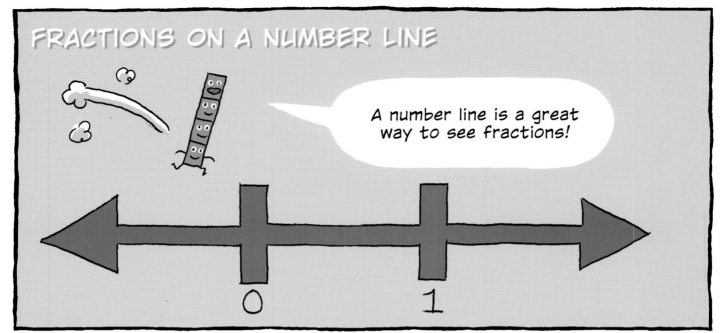

A number line is a great way to see fractions!

Here, we have the number 1.

In the real world, 1 can represent one thing, but here, it's just a number.

So, let's find 1/2 on the number line.

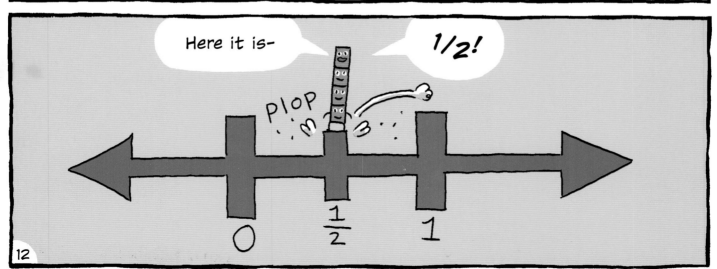

Here it is—

1/2!

plop

13

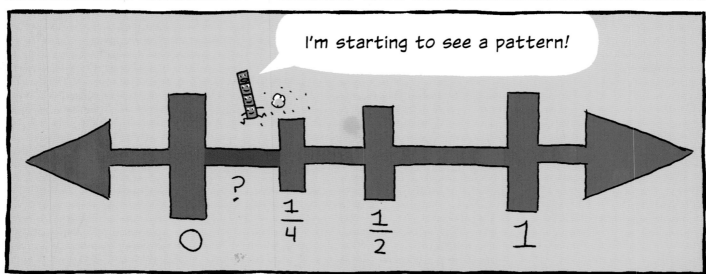
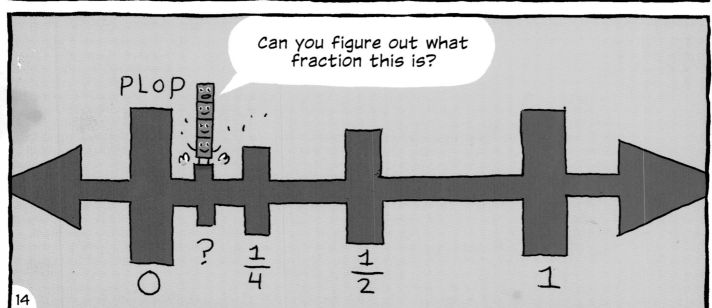

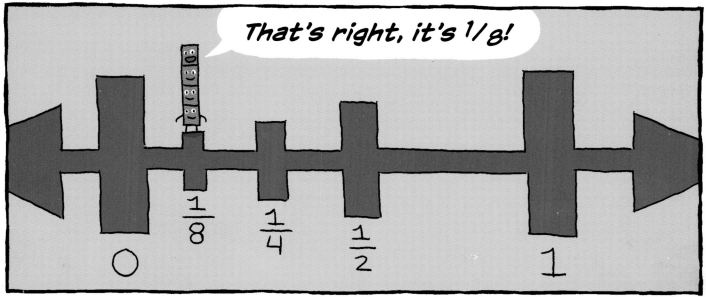

Now I have 2 slices of the whole pizza back in the box.

That's 2/5!

Uh, I don't care for sausage.

Now I have 3/5 of the pizza.

PLOP

I'm not a big fan of olives.

4/5!

PLOP

I don't even like pizza.

You guys sure are picky...

PLOP

5/5 equals the whole pizza!

I guess I just have to share all 5 slices with myself...

munch
munch
munch
munch
munch

PARTS OF A WHOLE

Spools of yarn!

And different colors, too!

Together, ALL of this yarn is a *collection*, or a *whole*!

But, some of the yarn is blue and some of the yarn is green.

What fraction of *all* the yarn is blue?

First, let's count up the whole collection!

There are 12 spools of yarn altogether.

1, 2, 3, 4, 5, 6, 7, 8, 9, 10, 11, 12.

That's our denominator!

?
12

Now, let's count up how many of the spools are blue...

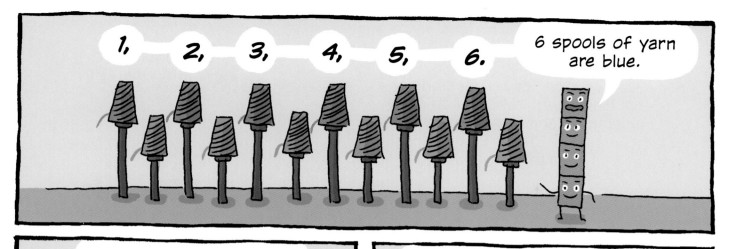

1, 2, 3, 4, 5, 6.

6 spools of yarn are blue.

That's our numerator!

$$\frac{6}{12}$$

So, $\frac{6}{12}$ of the yarn is blue.

Now, what fraction of *all* the yarn is green?

Remember, we have 12 spools in all, so our denominator is 12.

$$\frac{?}{12}$$

So, let's count up the green spools!

1, 2, 3, 4, 5, 6.

$\frac{6}{12}$ of all the yarn is green as well!

Knit Knit Knit Knit

Oh, brother...

Now, if only I knew how to knit.

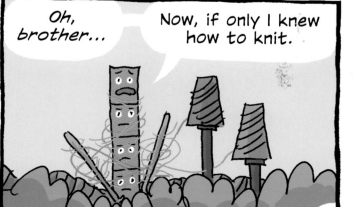

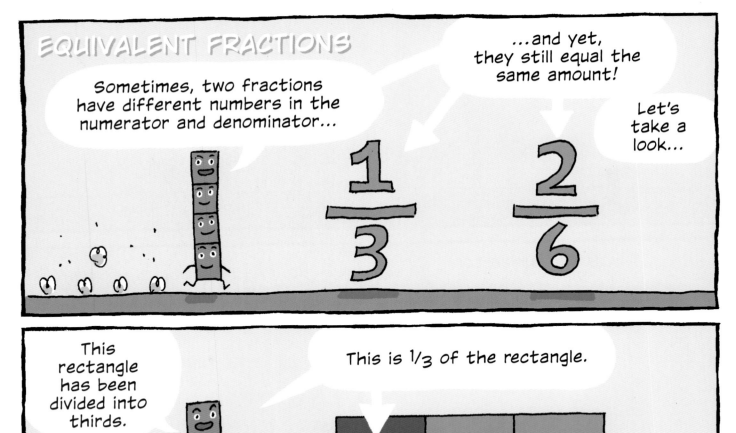

EQUIVALENT FRACTIONS

Sometimes, two fractions have different numbers in the numerator and denominator...

...and yet, they still equal the same amount!

Let's take a look...

$$\frac{1}{3} \qquad \frac{2}{6}$$

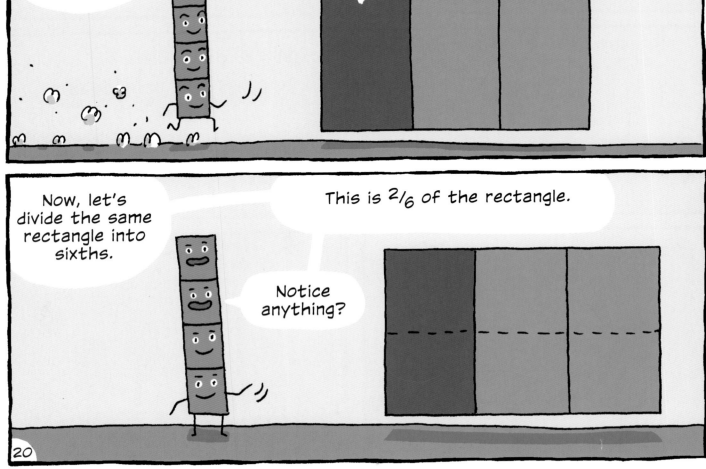

This rectangle has been divided into thirds.

This is 1/3 of the rectangle.

Now, let's divide the same rectangle into sixths.

Notice anything?

This is 2/6 of the rectangle.

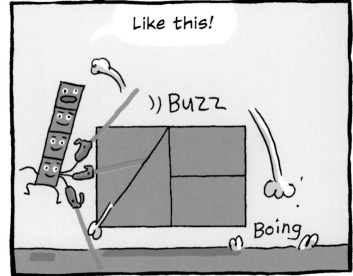

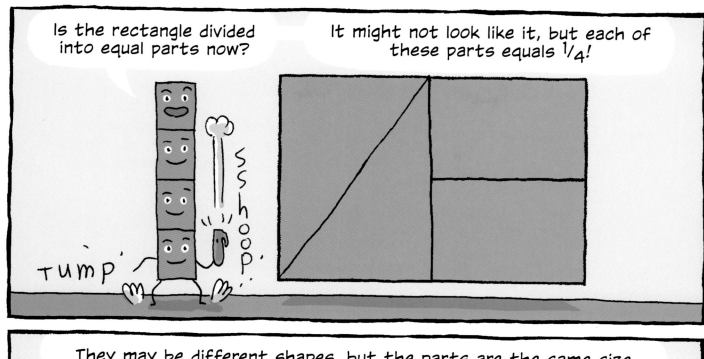

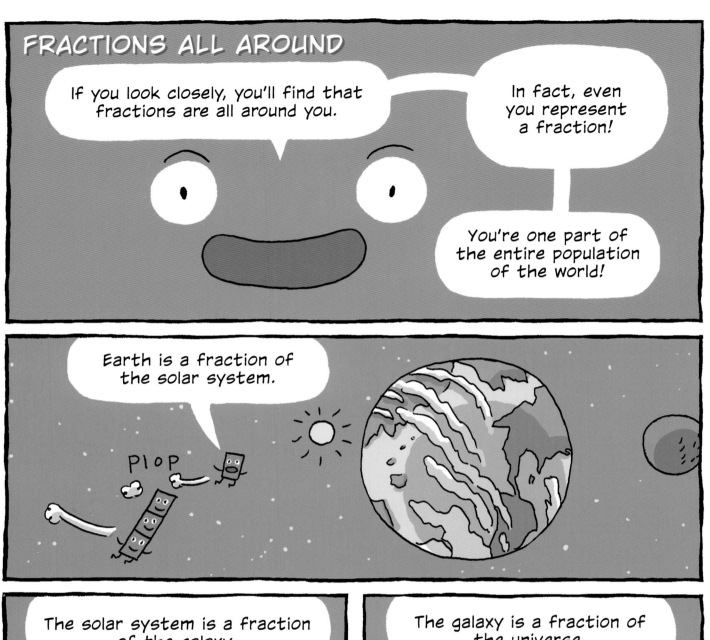

FRACTIONS ALL AROUND

If you look closely, you'll find that fractions are all around you.

In fact, even you represent a fraction!

You're one part of the entire population of the world!

Earth is a fraction of the solar system.

PLOP

The solar system is a fraction of the galaxy.

PLOP

The galaxy is a fraction of the universe.

PLOP

We are how you can describe all of these things.

So remember, if you ever need to describe an amount that is part of a whole...

...or, even a whole amount...

...use us!

We're Fractions!

29

FRACTION FACTS

The diagrams on this page can help you see several common fractions. Remember, fractions come from breaking a whole into equal parts.

FRACTIONS

FRACTION NAMES

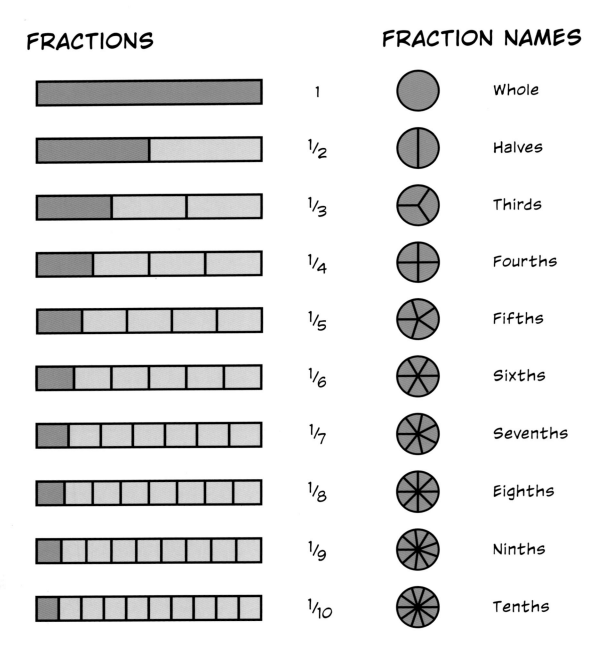

1	Whole
1/2	Halves
1/3	Thirds
1/4	Fourths
1/5	Fifths
1/6	Sixths
1/7	Sevenths
1/8	Eighths
1/9	Ninths
1/10	Tenths

FIND OUT MORE

BOOKS

Eat Your Math Homework: Recipes for Hungry Minds
    by Ann McCallum
    and Leeza Hernandez
    (Charlesbridge, 2011)

Fabulous Fractions: Games and Activities That Make Math Easy and Fun
    by Lynette Long
    (Wiley, 2001)

Fractions, Decimals, and Percents
    by David A. Adler
    and Edward Miller
    (Holiday House, 2010)

Fractions and Decimals Made Easy
    by Rebecca Wingard-Nelson
    (Enslow Publishers, 2005)

A Fraction's Goal: Parts of a Whole
    by Brian P. Cleary
    and Brian Gable
    (Millbrook Press, 2011)

If You Were a Fraction
    by Trisha Speed Shaskan
    and Francesca Carabelli
    (Picture Window Books, 2009)

Riddle-iculous Math
    by Joan Holub
    and Regan Dunnick
    (A. Whitman, 2003)

What's a Fraction?
    by Nancy Kelly Allen
    (Rourke Publishing, 2012)

WEBSITES

A+ Click
    http://www.aplusclick.com/
    arithmetic.htm
    Test all your different kinds of math skills with the games and practice activities here.

Cool Math 4 Kids: Fractions
    http://www.coolmath4kids.com/
    fractions
    Try out the lessons and practice games at this educational website.

Funschool: Number Games
    http://funschool.kaboose.com/
    formula-fusion/number-fun
    With games like Action Fraction, this site makes learning math a blast.

Math Is Fun: Fractions
    http://www.mathsisfun.com/
    fractions-menu.html
    This site has options for learning about fractions at many difficulty levels.

Melvin's Make-a-Match Game
    http://pbskids.org/cyberchase/
    math-games/melvins-make-match
    Help Melvin sort out his laboratory with your fraction skills!

PrimaryGames: Pizza Party
    http://www.primarygames.com/
    fractions/start.htm
    Use your fraction knowledge to figure out how much pizza is left for the party.

NOTE TO EDUCATORS

This volume supports a conceptual understanding of fractions. With the Fractions character as their guide, children are introduced to different representations of fractions, including set, area, and measurement models. Below is an index of concepts that appear in this volume. For more information about how to teach fractions in the classroom, see the list of Educator Resources at the bottom of this page.

Index of Strategies

Educator Resources

Children's Mathematics: Cognitively Guided Instruction
by Thomas Carpenter, Elizabeth Fennema, Megan L. Franke, Linda Levi, and Susan B. Empson (Heinemann, 1999)

Elementary and Middle School Mathematics: Teaching Developmentally
by John A. Van de Walle, Karen S. Karp, and Jennifer M. Bay-Williams (Harcourt, 2013)

Knowing and Teaching Elementary Mathematics: Teachers' Understanding of Fundamental Mathematics in China and the United States
by Liping Ma (Routledge, 2010)

**Young Mathematicians at Work:
Constructing Fractions, Decimals, and Percents**
by Catherine Twomey Fosnot and Maarten Dolk (Heinemann, 2011)